CUT
THE
NOISE

CUT THE NOISE

BETTER RESULTS
LESS GUILT

CHRIS **HELDER**

WILEY

First published in 2018 by John Wiley & Sons Australia, Ltd
42 McDougall St, Milton Qld 4064
Office also in Melbourne

Typeset in 11/15 Sabon LT Std

© John Wiley & Sons Australia, Ltd 2018

The moral rights of the author have been asserted

A catalogue record for this book is available from the National Library of Australia

Cover design by Wiley

Cover image © ezume images/shutterstock

Printed in USA

10 9 8 7 6 5 4 3 2 1

Disclaimer

Contents

About the author

Chris Helder is a communication expert and master storyteller whose presentations have radically transformed how thousands of people worldwide communicate with clients, customers, colleagues, family, staff and teams. He has been a professional speaker for 16 years and has given some 2200 presentations around the world.

He is the author of two Wiley bestselling books: *The Ultimate Book of Influence* (2013), which has been published in five languages, and *Useful Belief* (2015), which is one of the highest selling Australian business books of all time.

Chris speaks at conferences in the areas of communication, influence, human potential, leadership and mastering the face-to-face customer experience.

Chris lives in Melbourne with his wife, Lucy, and their three boys, Jake, Billy and PJ.

Acknowledgements

There are so many people to thank that I could not possibly name everyone. It always amazes me that so many of the ideas I speak about come out of random conversations. Thank you to everyone who has taken the time to talk with me about your ideas and passion to make the world a better place.

Special thanks to Lucy Raymond at Wiley for your continued support as we publish our third book together.

Thanks to Duane Kelderman for discussing with me the idea of core beliefs. I look forward to continuing to work on and expand these ideas together. You worked with my father, and getting an email from you is so much like getting one from him. I miss him and I cherish your words.

Thanks to Penny Ryan, my assistant, for all your collaboration, sharing of ideas and passion for the business.

Thanks to my mother, Carol Dey, for the inspiration of your Operation Babylift story. Also, thank you for your inspiration every day of my life.

Of course, the biggest thank you of all to my beautiful family. You put up with my hectic schedule and make it work. I love all of you more than I can possibly put into words.

Introduction

There is so much mental noise in our world today. Never before have we had so many options—things to look up, think about, worry about and, most of all, feel guilty about. It's really hard to be perfect.

Everyone else seems to be perfect, though. Everyone we know is smiling, laughing and partying, with a drink in their hand, or on holiday in some tropical paradise, parading the best version of their world for everyone to admire. It's all so exciting—but of course nothing is really as perfect as it seems.

We glimpse other people's lives through our phones and tablets. For the most part, we are genuinely happy for them. We want them to find love, to relish a family reunion, to celebrate a milestone with a great meal at a top restaurant. We are happy to share those moments with our friends. At the same time, we also like to be recognised for our own exciting life. It feels good when people like us. It feels good to be validated.

The problem is our life is not going to be perfect. In fact, there is often a big gap between reality and our projection of reality, and it is easy to feel a sense of guilt about not being able to bridge that gap.

In this media age, as people feel compelled to push out the best version of their lives to their friends and followers, this version can be a lot to live up to. We live in a world that is constantly barraging us with both information and the pressure of expectation in every area of our life, whether financial, business, relationship, parenting, family, friends or health.

Over the past 16 years I have presented to more than two thousand audiences on five continents. I have met countless people who are trying so hard to push through all the mental noise in their lives, to be the perfect parent, partner, husband, wife, employee or employer while at the same time staying perfectly fit and never ageing.

Much of this internal noise revolves around people's feelings of guilt because they are unable to live up to these expectations. They are working late and feeling guilty for not being home with their family. Or they are managing a household and not finding time to keep fit and healthy. They try to juggle their time between work, home and fitness, but in the back of their minds they know their relationship is suffering because they are so constantly busy.

My goal in writing this book is to share with you some ideas that shed light on how our desire to be perfect often actually prevents us from having an outstanding life.

I believe we need to focus on maximising every situation we are in.

Recently I was talking with a very good friend who shared with me his own story of guilt. It's a game he has no possibility of winning. He likes to go to the gym at lunchtime. Every day at 11:30 he thinks about going to the gym. Some days he decides he is too busy to go, then he spends his lunch hour feeling guilty about his decision. On other days he decides he will go to the gym, but while working out he is constantly checking his phone. He feels he can't focus on the workout, so once again he feels guilty about his decision.

I want to change this pattern that so many of us experience in one way or another. We have to stop beating ourselves up.

But how?

In this book I introduce an idea called '10 seconds of guilt... move on'. I hope you like it and can use it to help you enjoy your life more. It's about acknowledging a feeling that is not useful and then quickly moving past this feeling. There are studies that suggest that more than 90 per cent of the things we worry over and feel bad about either will never happen or are things we cannot change.

This idea has really resonated with my Australian audiences. So many people, both men and women, have come up to me and shared their feelings of guilt around their aspiration to be perfect. Women have told me of their need to be a corporate powerhouse, domestic goddess, great mother, wonderful wife, perfect friend—and still find time to do yoga, work out at the gym and call their mother-in-law. It's impossible!

Deluged by a media storm of news, fake news and social media messaging, we struggle to keep up. All that external noise creates a swirl of internal noise about what we should care about and how we should behave in our efforts to get it all right.

But the storm of information only convinces us of our many shortcomings. We must improve the quality of our lives, our business success, our health and fitness, our general happiness. Any failure to act makes us feel guilty. We need to lose weight, burn carbs, curb our sugar and salt intake, eat more superfoods! Sometimes it feels like the experts say one thing one year and contradict themselves the next. We are being marketed to so heavily it is driving us to overwhelm. The consistent message is that we must turn our lives around.

I hear a lot of motivational speakers at conferences seeking to convince their audience that they need to 'transform' themselves, to make massive changes in their lives. For most people, the prospect of personal transformation is overwhelming. In any case, the vast majority don't want to be transformed. There are exceptions in every audience, but most people do not want to invest the necessary energy and commitment to double or triple their output. They simply want to get the most out of the life they have in a way that is realistic and achievable. People have a lot going on. And that's okay.

My experience is that for most people useful, effective change is not about being transformed. Rather, it happens when people focus on a couple of things they want to adjust. When they are able to shift just a few of those stumbling blocks to their greater success, the trajectory of their lives and businesses changes dramatically.

I hope this book will help you identify some of the simple changes you can make to improve the quality of your life and to find the things you could start doing and stop doing to get there. Actually, you probably know what those things are already.

Cut the Noise begins with two fables (Part I) and goes on to explore some useful and I hope inspiring actions and anecdotes (Part II). I chose this format in part because I discovered through my previous book, *Useful Belief*, the power of fables in effectively communicating a message. Every reader will find ideas in this book they can usefully apply in their own life.

Our lives are made up of a patchwork of interactions with other human beings. In these two fables we hear a couple of conversations in which the speakers discuss their take on the challenges of life today.

In the first conversation, which takes place mainly in a Melbourne café, Will and Georgia discuss the concept of guilt in modern life and work. In the second, Noah catches up with his sister Sammy at her country wedding, where he discovers the keys to making useful changes in his life.

Through these two stories and the anecdotes that follow, I hope this book will set you on a journey of your own—towards self-awareness and a better approach to business and personal relationships. You'll learn how to cut out some of the things in your life that are not useful, to break through the stumbling blocks that obstruct your communication and action, to prioritise what is really important and to give yourself permission to make the most of every situation without guilt.

This is a book about cutting the noise. It's about focusing on the things that matter and freeing ourselves from the noise that holds us back. Cut the noise. Better results. Less guilt.

Be selfish when reading this book. Focus on what is important to you. If something doesn't resonate, turn the page. Take away the stuff that matters to you and will make your life better. And enjoy!

Part I
Fables

No more guilt!

This morning I was running late, so I grabbed the bundle of mail in my letterbox on my way out the door and just shoved it into my bag without a glance. Now I sat in my office and opened the top envelope. I felt a brief pang of anxiety as I unfolded the letter. It was the final invoice from the funeral home.

My grandmother was an amazing woman. Her energy was infectious. She was sweet but could also be a bit manipulative, though not in a bad way. She just always knew how to get her way, and even into her eighties nothing got past her. A life well lived had come full circle with this acknowledgement from the funeral home. A strange final step in a life that would live on now only in our memories.

My favourite memory of her was how she loved to dance, and she was really good at it. I was always jealous about that. I've never really felt comfortable cutting loose on the dance floor. I imagine that being able to dance really well must be the best feeling in the world.

Thoughts of my grandmother cutting up the dance floor were interrupted by a rap on my office door. It was our receptionist telling me that my 9 o'clock appointment had arrived.

Her name was Georgia and I was to interview her for a job as an external consultant to help us improve our productivity. Honestly, with family and funeral still uppermost in my mind, I really wasn't prepared for this meeting. I planned just to question her around what she did and how she thought she could help us. I guess I was winging it.

Georgia, wearing a tailored wool navy suit over a bright white shirt, exuded a sense of calm confidence. Her warm smile quickly melted the awkwardness that usually accompanies meetings between strangers. She seemed comfortable in herself, conveying a sense of knowing without a hint of arrogance. It was good.

I began to tell her about our organisation, and she listened intently. She asked if she could take a few notes and was soon writing furiously, then she stopped abruptly. I was making a point about the distractions our people were exposed to. It was something I often thought about. I tried hard to keep everyone away from office politics, game playing and general distractions. I was concerned that all this noise reduced their focus and attention.

'Tell me about the noise in your organisation. What is it exactly that distracts your people?' she asked.

I thought about it for a beat. I didn't mean it in a critical way, necessarily. It just struck me that people were often a bit scattered. There is so much to pay attention to today.

The truth was I too often felt distracted, by my phone, relentless email pop-up alerts, text messages, social media—all competing to send me off target. As I thought about it, I realised how easy it is to feel like you are 'missing out' if you are not always connected. Missing out on what I'm not sure, but definitely missing out.

'Well,' I replied, 'I suppose I think there's simply so much going on that sometimes it's overwhelming for everyone. It's not that the team have bad intent. Most of them show up every day set on doing a great job. I just worry that they lose focus on what is really important.'

As I heard myself speak, it struck home how bothered I was by this lack of focus. Personally, I often wasn't nearly as focused as I should be. For my team, I know they are distracted. Recently politics in the organisation had reared its ugly head and taken a lot of people off their game.

'I understand,' she said, and somehow I felt she did. 'That's really what I'm here for. What I do is help organisations work out the stumbling blocks that undermine their productivity.'

I looked at her and was convinced at that moment that she was going to know exactly what she was talking about. But I wasn't quite ready to think about my own lack of productivity this morning, and I thought a change of scenery might help me focus on this conversation.

'Look, I haven't had a coffee this morning. What say we get out of this office and head downstairs? There's a great café on the corner and we can talk about distraction, stumbling blocks and how we might do things better around here.'

She smiled and agreed. I grabbed my bag and my wallet and we walked towards the elevator.

'I'm sorry, Georgia. I actually am a bit distracted this morning,' I said wryly, all too aware of the irony given our conversation. 'My grandmother died last week. Her funeral was on the weekend and I was literally looking at the paperwork when you arrived. So I have to admit that I haven't done my homework on you. Maybe we could sort of start this meeting again?'

'Okay,' she said. 'I'm sorry about your grandmother.'

'Well, you know, it's not generally something that arouses a lot of sympathy. I mean, she was old, right? There's nothing surprising about an old person passing away. She had a spark, though, you know? A real spark. And it's like a light has been put out. It's probably not always like that with old people. Sometimes maybe the light goes out long before the end, but it was different with her. The light was still lit; it was on, right to the end. So when it did go out, well, there was a loss there.'

As the elevator reached the ground floor I realised I was sharing a lot with this person I had only just met. I felt a twinge of embarrassment, but then I made eye contact with her. She seemed okay with it, and it came to me in that moment that I had no one to talk to about this stuff.

'She sounds like an amazing woman. It doesn't matter what age people are when they leave our lives. It still hurts. We love them.'

We walked out into the buzzing Melbourne CBD, pulling our jackets close as the cold wind whipped around the building. In the café we chose a table near the window, perfect for people watching. The trendy café was loaded with character, and with 'characters'. The sun streamed in, just clipping our table and lighting Georgia's face as she smiled again.

'So, Will,' she began. 'Thanks for seeing me. It's clear you had a tough weekend and you were thrown this 9 o'clock meeting to start your week. I'd be happy to reschedule if you want.'

'No, not at all. Look, Georgia, you come highly recommended. So now we are here, tell me about yourself. What is *your* story?'

'Ha!' she replied. 'My story? Well, let's see. You've opened up to me this morning, Will, so I'm going to do something I wouldn't normally do in an initial business meeting. I'll give you some background on why I do what I do.'

'Great,' I said. 'This is my style. Let's lay it out on the table!'

No more guilt!

'Okay. Well, I was always someone who wanted to be there for other people. As a young girl, I was the one my parents relied on, and my friends too. I was probably a bit of a people pleaser, not that that's such a bad thing. I liked to make sure other people were okay and happy.'

'Sounds good to me.'

'Yes and no. As a young adult, this same need to be there for everyone else showed up in my work. I have always been a perfectionist too, and I'd get a little obsessed about everything having to be just so. I would work hard to make sure everything was right and everyone was happy with my work. Mostly, this was a good thing. It meant I did good work, met deadlines and mostly got along with everyone.'

'A perfect employee,' I declared.

She smiled. 'Maybe, but I also spent a lot of time focusing on things that, in the grand scheme of things, were really not that important. I became so obsessed with the little things in certain situations that I sometimes missed what was really important.'

'Right. It's easy to do. I think we all do it at times.'

'It is. The problem was I often felt guilty when I couldn't get everything done perfectly. I'd get distracted over some detail that really shouldn't have been my focus, then I'd feel frustrated when the big picture wasn't working out the way I wanted it to.'

Cut the Noise

As Georgia was speaking, I couldn't help but think of all the parts of my life that I might be managing better. I knew I wasn't handling things perfectly and I definitely felt guilty about not being in better control.

'I wanted to eliminate this feeling of guilt when I couldn't be perfect,' she continued. 'That's what it came down to. And I learned the valuable lesson that trying to be perfect holds us all back from having an outstanding life.

'I mean, I did all the things that society told me I was supposed to do. I was a very lucky woman. I had a good job, met a great man, got married and had two wonderful children. I was juggling all of those things and was busier than I had ever been. I was trying to manage work, a home life, personal time, friends and trying to keep healthy and fit.'

'I don't think I'm doing any of those things as well as I could be. This really strikes a chord with me, Georgia. I sometimes feel guilty about not making the most of all of those situations.'

'Exactly,' she said. 'So one day I was listening to some of my co-workers talking. One was feeling guilty because she was working late and not spending enough time with her kids. Another said she felt bad because she didn't have enough time to go to the gym. Yet another said she felt conscience-stricken because she had not been following her diet. Then it hit me. *No more guilt!*'

'How do you mean?' I asked, unable to imagine how that could be possible.

She pulled in her chair, centred herself and began. 'I became really fascinated with the concept of guilt. I learned that most people feel guilty about most aspects of their lives. Working with a lot of women, I was shocked by how many were struggling to be a corporate hotshot, the perfect mother, a wonderful partner, and a fit, healthy and attractive woman, while still finding time for themselves. It doesn't work.

'I mean, we live in a world in which women are expected to be all things to all people. So many women I knew were working late and feeling guilty about not being home. Feeling like they weren't doing a good enough job for their kids. Yet when they left work early to pick up the kids, they felt guilty for not spending extra time at work.

'Of course,' she went on, 'most working women also feel guilty about not being a good enough partner or friend. Most of all, though, they feel they don't devote enough time to their health and fitness, or simply to themselves. With so many family and work obligations, they don't have enough time to focus on meeting their own needs.'

'Yeah!' I chimed in. 'You know, Georgia, this is good. We are bombarded with all these images of what we are supposed to be today. Media. Advertising. Social media. Everyone puts out this perfect image of their perfect life, but it's not real. People post the good stuff. The media airbrush the bad stuff. The bottom line is we end up feeling bad about ourselves. I think men are not so different. We feel guilty for a lot of those same reasons.'

'It's interesting,' she said. 'Both men and women are assaulted by this internal noise that tells us we are not as good as we should be. We have been raised on this crazy idea that we have to find "balance", whatever that means. As if somehow our work and personal lives can be neatly reconciled to fit our nine-to-five timetable. For most people, there are times when work has to be a priority, and there are times when family and friends should take priority. I wanted to find an idea that would take away that guilt for both men and women. I wanted to help them cut all this noise.'

'Cut the noise. I like the sound of that,' I replied. 'So what solution did you come up with? Is there a way to do this?'

'There is. It's a technique you can use to deal with guilt. It's called "10 seconds of guilt... move on".'

'Okay, how does that work? Tell me more about it.'

'We need to acknowledge feelings of guilt,' she explained. 'It is important to recognise when we feel guilty about some event in our lives. But the reason the 10 seconds is important is that we have to get rid of the guilt quickly so we can focus on what we really need to.

'Guilt is not a useful feeling, especially in the context of feeling bad about the failure to meet an unrealistic expectation. And the research backs me up on this. Studies show that when people feel guilty about an activity they are not doing, they are less effective at the activity they *are* doing. In other words, if you feel guilty because you are taking time out for yourself, you don't maximise the value of spending that time on clearing your mind. Get rid of the guilt and you will be more effective.'

'Okay,' I said, 'I think I'm with you. But guilt can sometimes be a useful emotion. For example, if you have done the wrong thing, it is important to feel guilty about it. Children need to feel guilty about poor behaviour—that's how they learn.'

'Of course,' Georgia replied. 'But this is different. This is about maximising your human potential every day. You're right. It is important to feel guilt to learn a lesson, but there is a point beyond which it is no longer useful to continue to beat yourself up.

'Basically, if the guilt relates to one of two critical situations, then we should use the 10 seconds technique.'

'What are those two situations?'

'Well, the first is that we are feeling guilty about something we cannot or will not change. The second is that we are feeling guilty about failing to be perfect. The desire for perfection gets in the way of an outstanding life.'

'Talk me through them both.'

'Let's take the first one first. If I can't change the situation, there is no point in feeling guilty about it. For example, if I'm on a business trip and am in another city, there's no sense in my feeling guilty about not being at home. After all, I'm not at home and nothing I can do will get me home tonight. Therefore I am better off focusing on the work I have to do in this city. Ten seconds of guilt, move on—and get the job done. Feeling guilty doesn't help anyone. It doesn't serve my family and doesn't serve my client, especially if I am feeling distracted.'

'I agree.'

'The second one is we feel guilty about our failure to meet an unrealistic standard based on the idea that we should be perfect. It's not normal to be perfect. It's human to make mistakes and have imperfections. We do the best we can and learn from each experience.'

As she was talking, I couldn't help but think about how often I would criticise myself for not doing a perfect job in some aspect of my life. All that internal noise was not productive and was certainly not useful.

'What I do now is I help companies prioritise so they can focus on what is important. I've worked as a top executive, manager and partner in business. I've also gone through a journey on which I learned the most important lesson in business and life: I could and should *cut the noise*.'

I really liked where she was going with this idea, yet something was bothering me. 'But how do I know what is important and what is simply noise?'

'Simple!' she said with a smile. 'The circles of importance.'

'That sounds daunting,' I laughed.

'It's actually very simple. I think of it like this. There are usually six major areas of importance in people's lives. They are family, work, friends, health, community groups and, perhaps most important, 'me time'. Put a circle around each of those words and they become your circles of importance.

'Now it's simply a matter of being aware of what your desired outcome is and focusing on what you need to do to accomplish it. If what I'm doing doesn't fit into one of my circles of importance, then it's probably just noise. Sometimes we just have to say 'no' to something that does not serve our circles of importance. I want to be aware of the actions, activities and areas of my life that are going to truly make a difference.'

Georgia's ideas had such congruency, and I realised I hadn't listened this intensely to another person in a long time.

'Wow,' I said. 'My head is ringing with alarm bells on all the things I do that I don't think fit into my circles.'

'It's so easy for us to find things that don't fit in our circles,' she continued. 'It's important to learn to say no. The ultimate message is *awareness*. The point is to be conscious. The idea that we can strike a perfect work–life balance is really just a myth. In fact, the idea actually creates needless guilt, because no one really experiences a perfect work–life balance.'

'I agree,' I replied, 'but there has to be some perspective. There have been many times when I have got things out of whack, with too much time focused on one of the circles, particularly the work circle.'

'The awareness part is everything. What is the most important thing to focus on right now? Prioritise that. Focus on that. I don't talk so much about work–life balance. Instead I teach a concept I call *accelerated focus*. When I know I need to focus on something that is important to me right now, I am going to really focus on it. Accelerated focus on that activity will give me better results.

'We live in a world in which we have come to celebrate the idea of multi-tasking. I hear people all the time bragging about their ability to do many things at once. But the research shows that accelerated focus—total focus on the activity for a period of time—will guarantee greater success at any task, whether it is sales prospecting, a workout at the gym or dinner with the family.'

'That's definitely true of my people,' I admitted. Listening to Georgia, I thought about the differences between the two concepts and how much more productive accelerated focus must necessarily be.

I started thinking about how this related to different times of the year as well.

'In my organisation, we have busier periods of the year when I need to be really clear about what I have to get done. I may spend less time at home, at the gym or "chilling out" than I would at other times of the year. In our more relaxed time, I can kick back a bit more. And I needn't feel guilty about taking my foot off the pedal when I'm on leave.'

'Right. It's called being on holiday!'

I laughed. 'I don't think I always do a very good job of that either. I'm the guy on the beach with his phone pressed to his ear.'

'We all do it,' she assured me. 'Remember, it's not about perfect. Perfection gets in the way of an outstanding life. It's about being conscious, awake to what is really important. Dial into those things and get rid of the noise in any given situation.

'Taking up a challenge with accelerated focus means you'll get better results. I hear people say all the time that they have to multi-task to get everything done. I know sometimes that's true. Sometimes we have no choice but to juggle several tasks at once. But people who multi-task constantly are being led by the events around them. People who attack a task with accelerated focus are in control of how they respond to the events around them ... '

Georgia broke off her speech-making and caught my eye with a self-mocking grin.

'Well, Georgia, we have solved half the world's problems this morning. You know what, off the back of this conversation I've just realised something I am going to do. I'm going to organise a dinner for my whole family. My grandmother's funeral was wonderful, but it was all so busy and I think most of us were pretty distracted. I want to have a little family tribute. A dinner with accelerated focus. No guilt about the past. No noise. Just a little celebration in her memory.'

Georgia had given me a lot to think about in that first meeting. I'm sure we'll get into the detail of how she will be able to help my organisation. But even in this short space of time she had introduced some simple but powerful ideas that could make a huge difference.

Cut the noise. I suddenly felt amazingly awake and aware of all the things in my life that make me feel bad about myself and distract me. Actually, that's it: It's really all about just being aware of what is happening around me. Am I in control of all the noise or am I overwhelmed by it? Am I allowing irrelevant external information to get in the way of what I really should be doing? Have I given myself permission to say no to things that are just distracting me from what is really important?

Key takeaways

10 seconds of guilt … move on!

There are two situations involving guilt in which this tool should be used. The first is when we feel guilty about something we can't control. If we can't control it or change it, then feeling guilty is not going to help us or anyone else. Take the 10 seconds to acknowledge the feeling of guilt … then move on. In the second scenario we feel guilty about not being perfect. We are all human, and sometimes things don't work out the way we want them to. We say the wrong thing, make a mistake. Take your 10 seconds and then ask yourself, 'What did I learn?' Get clear about that and leave the guilt behind.

Cut the noise

Today we are inundated with more stimuli, information and messages than at any time in human history, from traditional media to social media, from news (fake and real) to reality television, from email pop-ups to physical meetings with real people. And we are all busier than we have ever been. The challenge lies in determining what in all this interaction and messaging is truly important and what is simply noise that diverts our thoughts, time and actions. We need to eliminate the empty noise from our life.

An outstanding life, not perfection, should be our goal

Life is not perfect. When we are bombarded on social media with everyone else's best version of themselves, it can be hard not to feel like others are doing life better than we are. When we fail in our bid for perfection it creates a sense of guilt, because we feel that our actual life falls short of the version we aspire to. Our mistake is to focus on trying to be perfect rather than on living an outstanding real life. Allow yourself to do the best you can. You can't be a perfect parent, partner, employee and friend all at the same time. You can't maintain the same physical image you had 10 years ago. Allow yourself to be who you are. Be good to yourself and create an outstanding life.

Circles of importance

Creating an outstanding life is really about knowing what is truly important to you. Most people have six areas in their life that really matter. They usually include some version of work, family, friends, health, community and 'me time'. Throw a circle around those words and they become your circles of importance. Use these circles to prioritise what is important for you to focus on and spend your time on. If what you are engaged with does not fall into one of those areas, it is very possible that you are being distracted by the noise from what is really important in your life. Often other people convince us to focus on their agenda, which may well not serve us. It is so important that we recognise that it is okay to say no without guilt, or at least not more than 10 seconds of it! We all need to give ourselves permission to say no to things that are not working for us.

Accelerated focus

This technique will help you block out the background noise and give your current activity your full attention. Constantly assaulted by information from many different sources, and seeking to balance competing priorities, we have had to learn to do many tasks at once. But multi-tasking does not work. Determining what we need to do now and focusing on that task without distraction will deliver better results. Many teenagers today study with their phone on while participating in multiple social media conversations that can potentially involve hundreds of other students. Employees today work with email pop-ups and text messages perpetually interrupting their thought patterns. It is not possible to deliver your best work when you are constantly distracted. Accelerated focus is about being aware and in control of your focus in a world of distraction.

Food for thought

1   Which of these ideas resonated most with you? Why do you think that was?

2   What actions can you take in your life to reduce the guilt you feel about things you can't control?

3   What could you do in your life to reduce your need for perfection and help create an outstanding life?

4   Have you identified the core circles of importance in your life? Are you sometimes distracted by activity that clearly does not support those core circles?

5   How important is it in your life to get better at saying no to activities that do not serve you well?

6   We all have to multi-task to some degree, but do you often feel like you are trying to do too many things at once, and is that affecting your results? Do you sometimes feel out of control as a result?

7   How can you incorporate accelerated focus in your life? In what areas could you put this into practice right now?

Clear the stumbling blocks

2

I made a couple of last phone calls then stood up to stretch, glad to be done with work for a while. I had a big trip ahead of me this morning. My sister, Sammy, was getting married to a country boy from a little town that sits on the Victoria–New South Wales border called Tocumwal. The wedding would be held in his hometown, and quite a number of the guests would be making the four-hour drive up the Hume Highway from Melbourne for the celebration.

I was looking forward to getting away, and to the drive. It seemed like a long time since I had made a big road trip, and I was excited by the prospect. If I left in the next half hour, I should arrive in good time for lunch. I was meeting Sammy at 1 o'clock. The weather was tipped to be perfect, with clear skies and 27 degrees. I could relax and enjoy the fresh air, the scenery and the open road.

The trip through rural Victoria was spectacular. Big open spaces, the changing landscape burnished by the morning sunlight, majestic gum trees swaying in the wind. You would be hard pressed to find scenery more resonant of country Australia.

The last few kilometres of winding road told me the New South Wales border was only moments away. The feeling of exhilarating freedom and the temptation to accelerate through the curves were tempered by the sad clutches of dusty flowers and crosses on the side of the road marking where tragedy had struck. Sobering thoughts to check my excitement.

Finally the sign, 'Welcome to New South Wales', and I began to climb over the bridge. I glanced to my left towards the old railway bridge. Originally opened in 1895, the iron bridge has long been a landmark for this country stop on the magnificent Murray River.

I had arrived.

The little river town of Tocumwal is known to tourists for waterskiing, fishing for the famous Murray cod and a notable 36-hole golf course. Sammy had told me how much she loved it here. She had given me clear instructions. I was to meet her at the pub for a drink and a briefing on the weekend's events. The wedding would be the next afternoon, but she wanted us to spend some time together before the big event.

The pub wasn't hard to find. The Terminus Hotel is an imposing double-storey brick Victorian building with ornate wraparound verandas, loaded with local history. A few of the locals were enjoying a beer at the bar, but no Sammy. I wandered through the pub and took a few moments to study the photographs from the early 20th century. Those were tougher times and the sepia images

Cut the Noise

showed the hard men who had carved out a living on the river.

I followed the sign to the beer garden, where I found her sitting quietly by herself, scanning her phone.

'Sammy!' I opened my arms and drew her into a hug. 'How are you?'

'So good, Noah! It's great to see you. How was your trip?'

'Beautiful. Nothing like a country drive, is there? You know this though, don't you, marrying a country boy!'

'Thanks so much for coming up. It means the world to me that you'll be walking me down the aisle.' Sammy hugged me again. 'Welcome to Tocumwal, big brother! Let me go and buy you a drink. What would you like?'

'Cold beer on a hot day would be perfect.'

I watched her walk into the old pub. She looked great, fitter than I'd ever seen her. I knew she was planning on running a half marathon at the end of the year.

She strolled back into the sun-soaked garden with a cold schooner and a soda water with lime. She sat down and we raised glasses.

'Here's to you,' I said as our glasses clinked together. 'Feeling ready for all this? No second thoughts?'

'None. I'm so happy, Noah. Max is such a great guy. You know, I've struggled with all this relationship stuff for a long time. I am so glad I have this guy in my life.' Her smile was patently sincere and joyful.

'So I have to ask you, Sammy, what's the secret to the big turnaround? Marriage! You look great. I hear you're killing it at work. Is that true? Work is good?'

Sammy again flashed her beautiful smile. 'You know, Noah, it really has all come together. I mean, I used to worry about everything. It was really self-destructive. I'm sure it cost me business, cost me money. Ultimately it probably cost me relationships too. All that's changed.'

'That's awesome! Don't be too hard on yourself, though. I mean we all get anxious, stressed. We all worry.'

'I know we do, Noah.' She looked thoughtful for a moment. 'But then I came across this idea, and it just seemed to wipe out all that anxiety and noise in my head.'

'Hit me with it. What's this great idea?'

'Have a strategy for the stumbling blocks.'

'Stumbling blocks,' I echoed. 'Sounds right. Tell me about it?'

'Well, it's like this. I had this pattern of self-talk that would constantly trip me up. First of all, I would worry about everything that might go wrong. And when things did go wrong I would obsess about it. I was completely attached to the outcome of every single thing that happened to me, and I would self-sabotage and feel guilty when things didn't turn out perfectly.

'Then a friend of mine shared with me this idea about focusing on a strategy around stumbling blocks. It's actually the opposite of what so many people say. They say you have to avoid thinking about the problems and just focus on the goal. But I knew it was the stumbling blocks that kept tripping me up, preventing me from achieving my goals. It became very useful for me to have a strategy for dealing with the things that were holding me back.

'Let me give you an example. Let's take a goal like losing weight. Why do most people fail to achieve the dietary goals they set themselves?'

'Well, it's hard. Food is good!'

'Sure is. Okay, so let's say just for fun that you want to quit eating chocolate. The first thing you have to do is identify the *why*. Why do you want to quit this thing that's not working in your life? Once you've done that, then you have to focus on the stumbling block that's preventing you from achieving this goal and decide on a strategy. You need a strategy for that moment when you are going to be most tempted to eat chocolate.

'That's important. Anyone can set this goal first thing in the morning. But that's not when people typically want chocolate. You have to prepare for when it's going to be really challenging for you. For most people, that's probably 9:30 at night with a cup of tea. That's going to be the moment when Mr Toblerone begins calling you from the refrigerator!'

'I love Toblerone.'

'We all love Toblerone, Noah. Stick with me on this.' She smiled and took a sip of her soda water.

'This is what my friend shared with me: The key to accomplishing a goal is being prepared for all the things that are going to *stop* you. In a way, it may sound counter-intuitive. You have to plan for the bad things that could get in your way. Focus on your goal, but also have a plan to deal with the stumbling blocks. So with chocolate, have a plan for 9:30 at night. The plan itself is very simple. I call it the "when, then" plan. When that happens, then what are you going to do? When Mr Toblerone starts calling you, then what actions are you going to take?'

'Eat a carrot, I guess,' I replied glumly.

'Right! Now, I know carrots are not as great as chocolate, but if you've set a goal to lose weight, it might be a good strategy. It's the same with running. I used to exercise when it suited me. I never really had a plan. I would just fit it in when I had a little free time. So I applied the strategy to my running. "Why am I doing this? Focus on the stumbling block. When, then.' I was clear about why I wanted to start running, but I also knew how tempting it was to switch off the alarm and go back to sleep, because sometimes it's hard to get out of bed.'

'Almost impossible on a cold winter morning in Melbourne,' I agreed.

'Okay then, let's stay with running. You know why you wanted to start running. Anyone can go for a run on a beautiful summer morning. It's that cold, wet morning you need a strategy for. When, then. When it's cold and raining, then I am going to put my alarm on the other side of the bedroom with my running shoes directly beneath it. Strategy. Planning. But the most important thing is I'm planning for the stumbling block.'

'I like it, Sammy. So it was this planning for stumbling blocks that took away your anxiety?'

'Yeah. At first when my friend took me through this, thinking about the stumbling blocks made me worry even more. Again I was thinking about all the things that could go wrong. But then an amazing thing happened: once I had a plan for every challenge, my stress levels went down. I mean, when you are properly prepared for something there really isn't any reason to stress on it. Preparation eliminates most of the stress.'

'I can see that,' I said. 'I mean, if you look at an actor or a musician, if they are completely prepared, then it's really just about the performance. The stress would come if they didn't know their lines or didn't know the song.'

'So then, big brother, I discovered the greatest thing of all.'

'Hit me,' I smiled.

'I became more detached from the outcome. I was prepared for what might go wrong, and I had a strategy for dealing with it. That way I would know I had done the best I could. I used to get myself tied up in knots over every little thing. Now I think, we'll see. It won't do me any good to worry about things that aren't real or that I can't control. What will happen, will happen. It's the same with this wedding. The old me would have been worried about everything that might go wrong. Not now. I'm just excited about it. We've planned the best we can. We've even thought about getting around any unexpected stumbling blocks. Now we've done that, I sort of think, well, what will be, will be.'

As I was listening to her, I realised how much I needed to hear this today from Sammy. I have been so stressed at work lately, worried about the little things and not focused on what really matters. When she talked about the importance of understanding *why* we do things, it really resonated with me. I really didn't have a series of clear goals in my life. I was winging it from day to day. The truth was that in all those areas that Sammy was succeeding in, I wasn't at all happy in my own life.

'When I was more detached from the outcome of every situation,' she went on, 'I found I didn't need everything to be perfect. I had been running around vainly trying to be perfect at everything and just worrying and feeling guilty. I wasn't actually getting the job done. But now I don't need everything to be perfect. I really do believe trying to be perfect gets in the way of an outstanding life.'

'Wow.' I gazed at my beautiful sister as she spoke with such clarity about her new view of the world. 'I'm proud of you. I need to think about all this, though it has obviously really worked for you.'

'It has. And yes, it's been great with my job too,' she said. 'It was really all about cutting out all the noise of self-doubt and self-talk that simply wasn't useful.'

We took a breath, and I became thoughtful. My experience with simple formulas and motivational mottos had been less than successful. And if I'm honest, I have to admit that I felt a little jealous. The cynical part of me probably wanted to scoff at all this. But it's hard to argue with results. What struck me most was how calm Sammy seemed. Knowing how difficult the past few years had been for her, that's what really blew me away. *She was so calm.*

'I love all this and love what you are doing,' I began. 'There's really so many reasons for celebration. Listening to you, Sammy, I realise I've got to pull myself together. But ... I mean, of course everyone would love some simple tip that would change everything. I just think I have really sort of given up hope of ever finding such a solution. There haven't been any silver bullets in my life. I would love to think I could stumble on some idea that would make me happier. I have done all the things that are supposed to make your life better. I've read all the books, listened to the podcasts. In the end, when none of the promises delivered a result, I found that they all left me feeling a little empty.'

'I think you're missing the purpose,' she said. 'You're missing the *why*. Why do you do what you do?'

'Sammy,' I persisted, 'you know the sort of guy I am. I'm very practical. I manage a sales team. I've been to all of those seminars, and I can tell you I've rarely seen lasting change come out of a bunch of rah-rah. My team would go to these seminars and come back really fired up. The energy and motivation would last for a couple of days and then everyone would revert to the way they were before.'

'I hear you, Noah,' she said. 'I don't want to agree with you, but in the past I've had the same experience. I think most people go to a seminar and take lots of notes that end up filed away and forgotten. But a couple of things were different this time for me.'

'Go on.'

'First of all, I realised something. The things I had done in my life that I was most proud of were *hard*. They took a lot of work. Second, I recognised that I was living well within my comfort zone, and no one has ever achieved anything they are really proud of without breaking out of their comfort zone. Then, most of all, I realised that I feel most alive when I'm having a go at something, when I'm focused on work or training to run or throwing myself into this relationship. And I love feeling alive!'

That was it. I knew she had hit it on the head. I wasn't pushing myself, so I wasn't feeling alive. I was consumed by the noise.

'You know what,' Sammy continued, 'I read this article about the human brain and how its purpose is to protect us. For hundreds of thousands of years, our brain has tried to keep us safe, to keep us in our comfort zone.'

'I'm sure that's true, but it did mean we didn't get eaten by crocodiles!'

She laughed. 'I know, but for me it was important to tell my brain that I wanted to be *alive*. I wanted to be put in situations where I would push myself. In the past, those situations would only have made me worry and feel anxious. But now I'm embracing these feelings. I'm aware of how I feel. I plan for the stumbling blocks that might come up and I cut out all the noise in my head. I want to stay a little detached. Let's see what happens, and no matter what happens it will be okay!'

'You're right,' I said. 'I certainly need to get rid of some of the noise inside my head. And I think there's more noise when I stay inside my comfort zone. My goodness, Sammy! That may be enough analysis for one day. Congratulations!'

She smiled and once again we tapped glasses. She had given me a lot to think about.

'Okay, so what's the plan from here?'

'Get yourself settled in, then tonight is the barbecue on the river. You'll love it. It will be so much fun. I'm excited for you to get to know Max. He's a great guy.'

'I can't wait. He's a lucky man, Sammy.'

* * *

The barbecue went off perfectly. Family and friends gathered to enjoy the warm early autumn evening and celebrate the occasion. I had a chance to meet Max's parents, who were good country people, farmers who worked and loved the land along the Murray River. Conversation and laughter flowed easily.

Most amazing to me was how the colour of the river kept changing, the reflections of the trees and the orange hues of the sunset making this ever-changing canvas almost impossible to look away from.

The one person I hadn't had a chance to catch up with yet was Max. As the night wore on, he was deeply absorbed in conversations with his family and childhood friends. Dinner was long over when I found Max staring out over the water. Max was tall and carried himself like someone who knew where he was going yet was not necessarily in a hurry to get there. I think Sammy liked that about him. He brought calm into her world.

'Max,' I interrupted his thoughts, 'I'm sorry we haven't had a chance to talk. What a great group of people! Beautiful family. Fine friends. Everyone has made me feel welcome. Thanks for that, mate.'

'Of course, Noah. We're family now.'

So our conversation began. He talked about growing up on the farm, lessons it taught him and what his childhood had been like, referencing many of the people who were with us here by the river. I was struck by his manner. He really did seem like he was very happy to be here, in the moment, talking with me. His speech was slow, steady and congruent. He was very impressive. With all that talk with Sammy about planning, stumbling blocks and living outside our comfort zone, I couldn't help but be curious about what made Max tick.

'Max, can I ask you a personal question?'

'Sure. I am about to marry your sister, after all.'

'You seem very deliberate. Like you know what you are doing in every moment. I don't think I feel that way a lot of the time. I think often I'm just reacting to what's going on around me … What's your secret?'

'Secret?' He laughed. 'I don't think there's a secret.'

'Well, this may be too personal, but you seem like such a present person, not distracted at all. Do you actively remind yourself to be present?'

He leaned back and took a drink. With a little smile playing at the corner of his mouth he replied, 'Well Noah, I've always thought about it like this. I believe everything we do in our lives is for one of three reasons: love, money or accomplishment.'

I was surprised his answer was actually that clear.

'Tonight, for example, is about love. I love everyone here. So, I don't have any attachment to an outcome for tonight. I just want to spend time with these people. I frame up tonight in the "Love" category. It's about having fun. I don't need to win anything or be anything I'm not. Just enjoy the company.'

'Wow,' I said. 'That is a really cool frame for tonight. I don't think I've ever walked into a social setting with this level of clarity.'

'Well mate, every situation is different. Earlier in the week I was at work and I'll be honest, I had to do some things as part of my job that I don't like to do. We had made some mistakes and the paperwork was ridiculous. But it had to be done. I didn't need to love it. So what I do is I frame that up in the "Money" category, and that helps me. I see a lot of young people today who think they need to love every minute of their life. If you frame everything up as love, then you become a little frenetic about constantly needing to find joy in every moment. Not everything has to be fun. Not everything has to give us joy. This was work. It's what I do for money, so I frame it up like that.'

I had never heard someone break it down quite like this before. Max had a way of delivering his thoughts so you found yourself hanging on every word.

'Sometimes,' he went on, 'I'll do something that I don't particularly love and that doesn't make me money. I may help a mate build a new fence, for example. Now hopefully we can have some fun doing it, but that's not the outcome. The frame is accomplishment. We've got a task in front of us. We need to do it. So I put it in the "Accomplishment" frame. When I frame it up like that, I don't get upset if it ends up not being fun. Also, I certainly don't want money for it. I want to help my mate. It's just about the accomplishment'.

'That's awesome,' I said. 'Love, money and accomplishment. So simple.'

'Keeps me focused on what I'm trying to do.'

'Max,' I said. 'So great to talk with you. I think you're a lucky man marrying my sister, but she's pretty lucky too.'

I had a few more casual conversations and tried to focus on the 'Love' frame for those conversations. When you frame up a party conversation as love, it's amazing how easily it flows without your needing to try to impress the other person. The conversation just happens.

With my mind whirling with new ideas I decided to take a little walk along the river. The vibrant colours of sunset had been succeeded by dancing moonlight, shimmering on the fast-flowing water. What a day it had been! Sammy had taught me about understanding the importance of knowing why you want to do something, eliminating stress and worry by focusing on the stumbling blocks, and having a plan. She had also challenged me on the danger of staying inside my comfort zone, and how truly alive we feel when we are pushing towards something special.

I wondered, what would I start doing and stop doing to make this the best year of my life? What would make me, 12 months from now, feel proud of what I had done? It was clear to me that I would need to move outside my comfort zone.

Then that great conversation with Max, who framed up the activities in his life in terms of love, money or accomplishment. I thought this was an incredibly powerful idea. And he had a great point about work. Not everything has to be fun; sometimes it just has to be done.

The next couple of days were amazing. I walked Sammy down the aisle and she and Max rode off into the sunset together. It was quite a moment. The weather was glorious and Sammy smiled all afternoon long. It was perfect.

As for me, I framed it all up in the 'Love' category. Pure joy.

* * *

Sammy and Max taught me about cutting out the noise of life, and that's just what I have done. I had so often brought up work topics in social settings that should be reserved for love, rambling on about my job at a dinner party to the discreet boredom of my friends. I definitely made the mistake of obsessing about how a task is not fun when it simply needs to be done, to be finished. It was seriously important for me to be reminded that not everything has to be fun. From now on, I am going to be framing up all the activities in my life. This will help me to be absolutely clear on what I want to achieve. Then I'll just enjoy each moment without being attached to the outcome.

Key takeaways

Focus on the stumbling blocks

Once you are clear about your goal, ask yourself, 'What are the things that are going to stop me from achieving it?' Work out a strategy on how to attack and conquer each of those stumbling blocks.

Devise a 'when, then' strategy

To deal with those stumbling blocks, think 'when' that happens, 'then' I will do this. Applying an effective strategy to deal with stumbling blocks will ultimately reduce the anxiety and worry in your life. Preparation reduces stress.

Don't get too attached to the outcome

If you have set your goal and done all the preparation you can, then the best way forward is to not get too attached to the outcome. Notice what is happening, learn and adapt. The outcome will be as it is. What can you do better next time?

Break out of your comfort zone

When you are really alive, you are challenging yourself. Nothing amazing will ever be accomplished from within your comfort zone. Think of the things you have done in your life that you are most proud of. Notice how they all challenged you, demanding that you step outside your comfort zone. What would you do this year if you were going to do something amazing?

Love, money and accomplishment

This is a tool to help you get clear about your activities and goals. Frame up every activity in your life in a love frame, a money frame or an accomplishment frame. This will help you find your why. It will increase your focus and give you a greater sense of satisfaction in all you do. Not everything we do has to be fun.

Food for thought

1   What are the stumbling blocks in your life that have kept you from the goals you want to achieve? In business? At home? In health and fitness?

2   How can you apply the 'when, then' strategy to your stumbling blocks? Write down some strategies you can use to overcome some of these obstacles.

3   What are your thoughts about not getting too attached to the outcome? Do you get so attached to a result that you fail to see other opportunities? Care, but not too much.

4   Do you always stay inside your comfort zone? If so, what would persuade you to take a risk to achieve something great? We are most alive when we are pushing ourselves.

5   What are your thoughts about 'framing' each experience in your life to gain clarity? Do you fall into the trap of needing every experience to be fun? How will framing help you to attack difficult tasks at work?

Part II

Actions and anecdotes

Purpose: Guilt takes a backseat to purpose

3

Purpose helps eliminate guilt and will help you gain clarity about what is most important in your life. This is a story about a woman named Carol Dey and a life-changing decision she made when I was very young. She also happens to be my mother.

In 1975 I was five years old and my little brother was two. That year my mother, a nurse, and a friend decided to travel to Saigon to help rescue orphan babies from the maelstrom at the end of the Vietnam War. They were part of a rescue program called Operation Babylift, which organised the evacuation of thousands of infants and young children from South Vietnam and helped with their adoption in Australia, the United States and several other countries.

It is an amazing story. Two nurses from middle America fly to Saigon shortly before the beleaguered city fell to the North Vietnamese Army and the Viet Cong. They smuggled money into the country for supplies, endured the very real threat of bombing and helped load jet planes with cardboard boxes containing hundreds of babies. They co-wrote a book on their adventure, which also featured in books and documentaries on Operation Babylift.

It was a dangerous journey. As I got older and had children of my own, it occurred to me to wonder how she could have taken such risks knowing she had two little children who needed her at home. As a father myself, I have tried to imagine a scenario in which my wife Lucy comes to me and says, 'Hey, would you mind looking after the children while I go to a war-torn country to rescue orphan babies?'

That would have been a really interesting conversation.

I asked my mom about it. Did she feel guilty about leaving us, given how dangerous the trip was likely to be? And it was certainly dangerous. The operation's first planeload of babies exploded shortly after take-off, killing 155 passengers including volunteers and babies.

One of my earliest memories is of the frantic phone calls seeking confirmation that my mom was not on that flight. By good fortune she was not. But she did describe the black smoke that erupted from the wreckage, and in the chaos I'm sure she was frightened, not knowing if the plane had been deliberately brought down.

Mom and her friend left Saigon days later in another aircraft with more than 200 babies lined up in cardboard boxes. All the volunteers had worked around the clock to care for the babies as they awaited official approval for take-off. The flight went without incident, apart from the continual need for hundreds of nappy changes.

Eventually they arrived safely in the United States where they were greeted by a team of volunteers and excited adoptive parents. Operation Babylift rescued more than 2700 children and brought them to new homes mainly in Australia and the United States.

When I asked my mom that hard question about guilt, she told me about an incident during her flight from Guam to the Philippines. It was the middle of the night, and the closer she got to Saigon, the more panicky she felt. In truth, she was terrified. Walking through the cabin, a flight attendant noticed she was wide awake and visibly shaken.

He stopped, leaned down and took her hand. He smiled at her and asked how she was doing. For some reason my mom opened up to him. She told him how she felt physically sick. She worried about dying, and she reproached herself for not listening to her family, who had warned her against making this trip. She told him how scared she felt as the prospect of landing in the middle of a war took on a greater immediacy.

She recalls how calmly he spoke as he told her that she was in fact more courageous than she knew. Most people would not have been able to overcome the pressure of family members' disapproval. That was courage, he said.

What he said next got her centred on the purpose of the trip. He asked her why she got involved in volunteering to begin with. My mom talked about how rarely anyone has a chance to truly make a difference to the lives of many, to change lives forever. To that, as she tells it, he replied, 'If you want to be strong, you will be. Just believe it.'

My mom said she instantly felt a sense of calm. She knew she was going to be okay. She knew her children were well taken care of at home, and she no longer felt guilty about leaving us. For the rest of the journey she was empowered for the task at hand, and she never felt scared or guilty again. He had helped her cut the noise.

As she tells it to me, when she got to Vietnam, she came alive. This conversation had refocused her on the reason she had decided to do this in the first place. Having purpose takes away fear and guilt. With the purpose in place, it is easy to focus on what needs to get done.

We can all think about what we want to achieve in our lives. What is the purpose that drives us to accomplish great things and embark on real adventures? To this day my mom recalls this adventure with pride as one of the most cherished accomplishments of her life.

Sometimes it is important to cut the noise and reconnect with why we started doing something in the first place.

Food for thought

1   Are there areas in your life where you could usefully redirect your thinking to why you started down this track in the first place? What was your purpose? Is it still your purpose?

2   Are there goals, dreams or adventures you have held back from simply because of fear or other people's criticism?

3   What goal are you pursuing that you can now no longer feel guilty about because you know it is important for you to achieve that goal?

Perfection: Real is better than perfect

4

In today's world we are perpetually hammered with the idea that we have to be perfect. It is not a useful message.

Advertising tells us the sort of body we should have, products we should own and experiences we should be brave enough to embrace. It would be easy to say that it has always been like this. There have always been beautiful people, products and lifestyles that were widely envied but virtually unattainable for the majority.

The difference today is we get a chance to do our own advertising. Social media has given everyone the opportunity to broadcast their life to the world. This is exciting, because we can share our greatest moments and get direct feedback on them. We can snap and upload holiday pictures of our pool view, cocktail, beautiful meal and beach walk, just like celebrities.

I have to say that I really enjoy most of it. It's fun to see what the people we care about in the world are doing. I live in Australia, and my mum can instantly see the pictures of our Thailand holiday from her home in Colorado. So it's mostly really cool.

There are two things to be aware of, however:

1. Needing your life to be perfect creates a massive amount of anxiety.

2. Comparing yourself to others creates a massive amount of anxiety.

Cut the noise. Double and triple check with yourself that your self-esteem is not completely attached to the number of 'likes' you get on social media. None of us are perfect, and in fact perceived perfection is actually not an attractive quality. It is easy to resent people whose lives seem too perfect. We are much more attracted to a level of vulnerability in people that makes them real to us.

People often ask me to talk about trends in selling and communication skills. Obviously, technology is always at the forefront of these trends. But what is out front on the human side of business? I have no hesitation: authenticity.

Be real. The more social media reflects your true self, the less stressful it will be. The further it moves away from the real you, the more attached you will be to the feedback you get.

I have spoken with many business owners who become stressed when they watch what their competition is doing. They become obsessed with their competitor's social media posts and quickly lose focus on their own business. Use social media and internet research time on your competition to generate new ideas, not to create new levels of panic and anxiety. Who knows, you may be able to replicate and actually improve on some of their successful activity!

Food for thought

1   Do you ever let social media affect how you feel about yourself? Is your need for affirmation from social media posts a healthy thing? If not, you need to cut the noise.

2   Are you judgemental of others on social media? Do you feel like you compete with others in an unhealthy way? Once again, there may be noise around how you view yourself as opposed to everyone else that is not useful.

3   Could you do a better job using social media to learn about and improve what you do in your everyday life?

Outcomes: We'll see what we see

5

I tried to be a perfect dad...but I got too attached to the outcome.

I have often taken everyone else's fun too seriously. In fact, many times in my life I have been guilty of being too attached to the outcome of other people having a good time. If you come to a dinner party at my house, I can be fairly obsessive about making sure everyone is having fun. I like to know that everyone's drink is charged, the food is good and the conversation is flowing. That's me. I love to entertain and I love it when people are having a blast.

Now, that's a good trait on the whole. But I want to say a couple of things about it. First of all, if taken too far it will set up a need for the night to be perfect. And perfection, as we have already established, gets in the way of an outstanding life. It can also get in the way of an outstanding dinner party.

So it is important for me to be aware that this dinner party doesn't have to be perfect. I can set it up so there is the potential for everyone to have fun. Then I need to let go and experience the night. What will be, will be. It's important for me to maximise my enjoyment of the evening and not to get too attached to the outcome.

Sometimes kids understand this better than adults. This was illustrated for me beautifully by my son Billy during a trip to Disneyland when he was five years old. You see, I had this idea that I thought was really cool. Since I'm from the United States, I thought it would be a great idea to take each of my three sons over there when they were five years old, just the two of us, to see my parents and go to Disneyland.

It worked out pretty well. I took Jake and Billy back to see my mum in Colorado and then to meet my dad at Disneyland in California. By the time it was PJ's turn my dad had passed away, and PJ wanted all of us to go on his trip. So we did. My mom loved having us all there and we did the trip to Disneyland together. Tick. Those trips gave me great joy and many memories.

When I took Billy, my middle son, to Disneyland it was just the two of us who made the trek over the Pacific to see my parents. We stayed in a hotel together in Anaheim with my dad and my stepmom and the next day, a bright sunny California morning, we ventured out to experience the 'happiest place on Earth'.

The day was amazing. Billy had a blast and was particularly excited by the parade. He was going through his Lightning

McQueen phase, and I don't know that I have ever seen such joy light up a child's face as when the full-sized Lightning McQueen came around the corner.

Earlier in the day, though, I had found myself too attached to the outcome of making sure he was having fun. We were in line for the 'Finding Nemo' ride and I was hyping the ride instead of enjoying the moment.

'Billy, how cool is this going to be! We're going to see Nemo! I bet we see Crush the Turtle too. Who knows? Dory is probably there as well, what do you think?'

He looked up at me and put his hand on my elbow, as though he felt sorry for my need to make this moment great, and said, 'Dad, let's just do the ride. It will be fun. We'll see what we see.' And he looked away.

Out of the mouths of babes!

We'll see what we see. Ten years later I still think about it all the time. It is something I say to myself in all sorts of situations. In fact, our entire family now recite it whenever we are about to embark on an adventure with an unknown outcome.

This year I was speaking in Thailand and my family joined me for school holidays after the event. The highlight was to be a 45 km family bike ride. We were at the Burma–Thailand border, all set for our adventure of biking down to the Gulf of Thailand. We looked at each other and said, 'As the great Billy Helder said, "We'll see what we see"!' It has become a family mantra.

We pedalled off with the right mindset. It doesn't need to be perfect. Let's just open our eyes and see what we see.

We could all be better as adults if we plunged into our next holiday adventure, dinner party, football game or family picnic without being completely attached to the outcome.

Care, but don't care too much. Don't get too attached to the outcome. We'll see what we see.

Food for thought

1   Do you get obsessed with the idea of pleasing others and ensuring everyone else is happy?

2   Are there times that you need to stop thinking about creating perfect outcomes for others and just let the event play out? Whether it is a dinner party or a family vacation, sometimes we have to just let things roll as they will. There is only so much we can control.

3   Would you enjoy these situations more if you reminded yourself that you have set them up as best you can, that now it is time to 'see what you will see'?

Identity: Core beliefs and identity

6

One afternoon in Byron Bay I collected my thoughts about 'core beliefs' and 'identity' and how they make 'useful beliefs' work even better.

I pulled into the parking lot at Wategos Bay. I had presented at a conference in the morning and decided to take some time this afternoon to write and to enjoy this magical part of the world. Travelling around Australia is pure joy. It is such a beautiful and wonderful place to live my life, and though it would once have seemed so unlikely that I would end up here, I am so grateful.

I had just been up to the lighthouse, the easternmost point of Australia, and had spent 45 minutes staring out over the ocean. The sun was shining and the water was electric blue, a colour I couldn't even begin to describe. Walking around the lighthouse I felt like I was a part of something incredible. I felt in awe of the world around me and had a sense of gratitude about the journey that had shaped my life. It is joyful to be awake and aware of the awesomeness around us.

Sometimes I worry that we are losing our ability as a society to be in awe of natural things. It may be a cliché to say that we need to stop and smell the roses, but it is worrisome that most people don't take enough time to take in the beauty that surrounds us. It's not easy, though. Why does it seem so hard to stop, look around and take it all in? Why is it so hard to pull ourselves away from our continual technological stimulation?

Firstly, we are busy. We love to tell each other how busy we are. It is usually the first thing out of our mouths when we see someone we haven't spoken to in a while. Of course, most people are incredibly busy. Society is busy. From the hustle and bustle of modern traffic to meetings, schedules and deadlines, most people are often on the verge of overwhelm from the sheer amount of activity they need to keep abreast of.

Secondly, we communicate all the time, and at record speed. Our dependence on social transactions through text, email, messenger, Instagram, Snapchat and Twitter means that we are constantly thinking about sending, receiving, responding and seeking feedback on our communications.

Thirdly, we are physically, literally, looking down more than ever before. Looking down a train carriage, it is normal to find the overwhelming majority of passengers staring down at their phones. Very few people are interacting directly with each other, and fewer still are consciously looking out of the window and taking in the surrounds. Don't get me wrong, I am doing the same thing. Mobile phones are absolutely amazing, incredible mini-computers. We have more technology in the palm of our hand than Apollo 11 had for the first moon landing. It is not easy to pull yourself away from that.

And yet there is a case to be made that this has not brought us happiness, and that most people are more miserable than ever.

Is it not the case that we all need to cut a little of this noise and take more time to connect with the awesome world around us? That we need to get less connected, and by doing so, become more connected to who we really are? How many people have a core belief that they are truly connected to nature? How many, I wonder, would like to? If you identified as a person who was truly in awe of the beauty around you, how would that help you start your day differently?

At Wategos Bay, I grabbed my towel and a notebook from the back seat and went down to the beach. I splashed on some sun cream, though I was pretty sure I hadn't done a very good job. I walked up the beach, the warm sand squishing between my toes. It was busy but I found some space and spread out my towel. I had a few ideas that I wanted to jot down, so I got out my notebook and prepared to write. I wanted somehow to draw this connection between appreciating each day and the busyness everyone feels.

In the first five minutes, I found that I had written down only two ideas:

1. Core beliefs

2. Identity.

Then it hit me. Core beliefs and identity are the final step in cutting the noise.

There is so much media noise telling us what to believe in. Everyone has an opinion and the media just turns up the volume and creates debate in which the loudest voices often get the most attention. Buzzwords are used recklessly by media and political grandstanders who are bent on making a name for themselves and in the process inflaming extremism and intolerance.

With the media today pressing us to pick sides and react emotionally to almost every topic, we need to be wary of getting sucked into confrontational thinking. Young people often tell me they want to connect with a cause or purpose so they can make a difference. But under this confused media bombardment they can become less clear about what they really stand for as they search to make an impact in the world. It is essential to sift through the extreme messaging to find clarity about your viewpoint. At the same time, being open to other people's ideas has never been more important.

We are all influenced by the noise around us. I too can be sucked into the media messaging. I enjoy social media, news broadcasts, reality television and debates about health, religion, politics and social issues as much as anyone. Like most people I have been sucked into emotional reactions to heated exchanges with stubborn people whose views I disagree with.

It is important that we do not lose our ability to seek out common ground with one another. Concession and compromise are an integral part of creating a society in which we can all communicate with, appreciate and love one another. However convinced we are of being right, we should never stop listening to and sharing ideas with others.

It is critical to identify the core beliefs that drive your life. They will help you decide how to make decisions about how to deal with all the noise.

This is a subject that receives too little attention in these times. When I ask people about their core beliefs, people often don't know how to respond. If they do respond, they may cite their circles of importance—family, work, friends, health, community and personal time. That's not it.

Core beliefs are the fundamental principles we live by. They shape our useful beliefs and help form our identity.

They shape us into something nobler, more beautiful. Here are examples of five core beliefs that could improve the trajectory of your life and approach to each day:

1. We are the truest version of ourselves when we focus on love, not fear.

Fear makes us irrational and prone to exaggeration. It leads to our stereotyping people and situations and focusing anger on isolated incidents and events. Fear makes people act with simple-mindedness and base judgement that ends up putting them on the wrong side of history. In contrast, you are the truest version of yourself when you focus on love.

Authenticity around being that true version of yourself is such an attractive quality. One of the things I love about Generation Y (Millennials) is that they will not tolerate anything that is not authentic. They know if you are not genuine. My advice today is to be knowledgeable and authentic. Be real and know your stuff. The quickest way to make yourself expendable today is to be incompetent and inauthentic.

Focus on the love in the world. In business, you will do the right thing by your customers. In life, you will form a wider worldview that serves people.

2. Gratitude produces more to be grateful for.

I have so often thought about the sliding door moments in life. Walking through one door can change your life completely. I really did not know anything about Australia when I met Lucy in a bar in Manhattan Beach, California. We were married seven months later and I have ended up living almost half of my life downunder.

How different my life would have been if I had decided to go somewhere else that evening! Could Lucy and I have met somewhere else? Would I still live in California? Would I be a professional speaker? The trajectory of my life could have been totally different. Sometimes it is fun to think about where the other sliding doors could have led us. Regardless, I love the door I walked through. I am very grateful that Lucy and I get to raise our three boys in this beautiful country. It is home for me now and I don't take the beauty for granted.

The more that you are able to tap into your gratitude and focus on the opportunities you have, the more of those opportunities you will begin to see. It is the same with the world that surrounds us. The more grateful we are for the natural world, the more beauty we begin to notice.

I live in Melbourne and people around Australia like to give my fine city a hard time about the weather. The great thing about Melbourne weather is its distinct four seasons. It is such a beautiful time in the garden when the promise of warmer weather is upon us and the spring buds first raise their heads. The more you notice the signs of spring, the more life and colour surround you. Gratitude produces more to be grateful for.

3. Forgiveness is critical to maintaining our personal health.

Much of the noise in our lives is not external but internal, and sometimes that internal noise can eat us up. So often we are trying to stifle the chatter of insecurity, regret, disappointment or anger towards someone who has hurt us. That noise can manifest itself in our identity and create a pattern of victim behaviour that is paralysing or destructive.

Bad things happen to everyone. We have all known pain and had experiences that left us feeling resentful towards someone. Those painful experiences will vary widely in intensity and in the damage they cause. I don't want to start a competition on degrees of suffering. Rather, I want to state simply that when we are able to forgive people, we feel better.

When we stop attributing blame, we are free to focus on becoming the best version of ourselves. It is very useful to recognise that other people can only do what they were capable of at that time. Managing your expectations of other people can help you manage your own ability to let things go. Give some thought to how you could do a better job of maintaining your personal health using forgiveness, managing expectations and letting go.

4. Giving to others is the key to our full humanity.

It is widely accepted that giving makes us far happier than receiving.

When we were children, receiving gifts was one of the most exciting things in the world. Holidays and birthdays were all about *us*. There was nothing quite like that feeling of opening our presents. Children, of course, are self-indulgent by nature. As we evolve into contributing adults, this need to receive should diminish.

Giving to others is the key to our full humanity. As adults, it is the giving that makes us happier, that makes us whole. This is going to mean something different to each person, but it is a good core belief. Guided by the idea that giving to others is the key to our wholeness, we find opportunities to contribute and make a difference to others.

And that makes us happy.

5. Life is purposeful.

Earlier in the book we discovered that having a purpose helps us eliminate guilt because it increases our conviction and confidence around making decisions. But it is much more than that. If you believe life is purposeful, you know life is important. Even if you feel like your purpose is not being fulfilled right now, believing that life is purposeful encourages you to find that purpose in your own life.

Sometimes I see speakers and facilitators get carried away on this subject. I see them challenge an audience about their purpose. I recently saw a presenter challenge a mother of three about what her true purpose was. The woman said, 'Paying the bills so I can raise my three children'.

This wasn't good enough for this presenter, who was clearly searching for a more idealistic answer. 'That's what you do,' he said. 'What is your purpose?'

She looked at him and shook her head. 'You clearly have no idea. My purpose until I get my kids through school is to pay the bills and be a good mother.'

She was right. That is absolutely what the driving purpose is right now. It will change in the near future, but let's live in the reality of now.

At the same time, studies show that most Millennials seek purpose in the company they go to work for. They want to make a difference in the world and to work for a company that has a positive social impact. Millennials want to learn, be mentored and spend time in organisations that have a greater vision and greater purpose. That is a good starting point to have as a core belief.

To believe there is purpose in life is to believe that what we do every day is important. That is a great core belief.

Identity and behaviour

These beliefs will help you find the true version of yourself. Our useful beliefs work better when they are aligned to a set of core beliefs. These beliefs are aligned to the rhythm of the universe and the wonder of being human.

They also help us find our identity and who it is we want to be. It is widely recognised that we behave in accordance with our identity. How you describe yourself determines how you behave. If you believe you are a fit person, you find your way to the gym. If you see yourself as a top salesperson, your behaviours will support this belief: you prospect, you pick up the phone, you create opportunities. If you see yourself as a good friend, you pay attention to what is happening in the lives of your friends.

This is especially apparent with parents. When they see themselves as responsible parents, they take the role more seriously. They spend time with their children. They get involved and attend their activities.

It is even true of confidence. At a nightclub a confident person who believes they are worthy of attention will attract more attention. How we see ourselves determines our behaviour and also how other people respond to us.

Recently my son PJ had to draw a self-portrait as part of a Year 6 project. He did a great job on the picture, but it was the next part of the activity that interested me most. At the bottom of the sheet of paper, he had to pick a word that best described him, while his classmates got to pick out a word *they* thought best described him. It was wonderful to look at this collection of portraits and see the positive adjectives picked to describe each child, wonderful affirmations that were so consistent with how these children saw themselves. It is no different for adults.

The opposite is also true, of course. If people describe themselves negatively, their behaviours will tend to match this self-description. They will often take the easier road. They won't push themselves and will look for excuses to take their foot off the accelerator. If they see themselves as unlucky, they will take fewer risks and stop pushing themselves towards a better life.

In fact, people who identify themselves in unproductive ways—as unattractive, uneducated, unlucky, unfairly treated, poor, unintelligent, a failure—will usually behave in ways that match these self-descriptions.

This is all noise. Cut the noise.

If you want to change your behaviours, it is important first to tap into the identity of the person you want to be.

For years, I have taught the concept of 'Act as If'. If you were going to be that person, what behaviours would you manifest? What would you focus on? What would you learn about? What would you read and watch? What would you start doing?

By the same token, what behaviours would you no longer demonstrate? What would you stop doing or focusing on? What would you stop giving energy to? What would you no longer read and watch? What noise would you cut so you could focus on the things that help you create the person you truly want to become?

Food for thought

1 What is your response to the core beliefs discussed here? How would your identity change if you adopted these core beliefs?

2 What are your own core beliefs? How would these beliefs change how you approach challenging social situations?

3 How do you describe yourself to others? How do you describe yourself to yourself? Are you happy with that? How would you like to be described? Act as if.

4 Do you find yourself reacting emotionally to media reporting, only to soften your stance later? What would help you sift through the media messaging and determine what is important and what is only noise?

5 Could you do a better job of being open to other people's viewpoints? Think of an example of this in your life.

Useful belief: The final step to cutting the noise

7

Useful belief leads to useful actions.

Two years ago I wrote my second book, *Useful Belief: Because it's better than positive thinking*. It was a great success. The premise of the book is that positive thinking doesn't work, but useful beliefs and actions do. This is the first part of the process of cutting the noise.

If you have been in a rut for the past 10 days, 10 weeks or 10 months, and someone admonishes you to 'be positive', you would probably want to punch them! Trying to be positive won't get you out of the rut. The real question is, what are the most useful actions for getting you from ground zero to two, from two to five, from five to eight and so on? Useful actions are pragmatic, practical; they are about executing a plan for success.

The idea of useful belief also ties in with what we see and perceive about the world. The book discusses the Reticular Activating System, which may be the most important part of the human brain when it comes to success. It is this system that filters the millions of pieces of information we receive every day.

I call this the Red Toyota Theory. Why? When you last took a drive, how many times did you see a red Toyota on the road? Answer? Probably zero. That's because you were not looking for red Toyotas. Now, if you decided to buy a red Toyota, where would you see them? Everywhere! The Reticular Activating System is the filter in the brain that determines what you pay attention to.

Your brain will find what you tell it to look for. The bottom line is that when you have a useful belief about something, your brain opens up so you see opportunities. If you believe this is the best time in the history of the world to be a parent, you will be a better parent. That's because you are focused on this year, right now, not on your own childhood. If you believe there are opportunities everywhere in your business, your brain will go find those opportunities. If, on the other hand, you believe these are tough times, your brain will find exactly that. Tough times.

Here are a few examples of useful beliefs:

- This is the best time in the history of the world to be alive.

- This is the best time ever to be in your industry.

- This is the best time ever to be at your company.

- This is the best time ever to be a parent.

- This generation of young people are exciting to be around.

- You had the parents and the childhood you were supposed to have.

- Everything that happened in your life happened for a reason.

- Life begins at ... [*insert your current age*].

There are obviously many more. This book was a game changer for a lot of people because it helped them deal with their reality. Two things will stop you from growing and getting better:

- complaining about things you can't control

- complaining about things you will not change.

You have created a certain life for yourself. You could change many aspects of that reality. As for those aspects that you're not going to change, you may as well have useful beliefs about them.

The example I often use on stage is the huge amount of travel I do. Last year I gave 153 presentations, which required 127 flights. That's a lot of flying! I could change this if I wanted to. Living in Melbourne, I could make the decision to restrict myself to Melbourne gigs. But that would affect my income and my lifestyle. So, if I'm not going to change it, I may as well have a useful belief about it. What's my useful belief about air travel?

I love planes! I love airports. I love airplane food. I am in hotels a couple of nights a week. I love hotels, hotel sheets. Being on the road I am alone much of the time. What do I love? Aloneness! If you are feeling lonely, *don't* feel lonely, dial in to aloneness. There is power in aloneness.

What aspects of your life are not going to change? Instead of complaining about them, create a useful belief about them. Then create some useful actions to follow through with.

I want to share with you two stories off the back of a couple of emails I have received.

The first was from a 28-year-old woman who had suffered from anxiety and depression all her life. As she told it to me, her family had urged her to be happier and more positive her whole life. But she didn't feel happy. She didn't feel positive. Then she told me she saw me on stage and I said, 'Positive thinking doesn't work', and she said she felt the weight of the world lift off her shoulders. She no longer had to be positive.

Three months later she called me and told me that an amazing thing had happened. She wakes up every day now and asks herself, 'What are the most useful things for me to do today to get through the day?' The result? She does those things and feels better about the process. 'Now I'm happier than I've ever been!'

Happiness isn't something to try to *be*; it is the result of living a full life.

The second email was from a man who had suffered an accident a year before that left him with burns covering a third of his body. He told me how he had spent the last year grieving over his injuries. Who could blame him?

The photo that accompanied that email showed him just out of surgery and holding a copy of a book he had been given — *Useful Belief*. He said that he was done grieving now. The grieving process was normal and had been useful. But there was nothing he could do to change what had happened, and now it was time to move on and to work on a useful belief for the rest of his life.

This is the first step to cutting the noise. We all have bad things happen to us in our lives. Some are devastating, like my email friend. His life will never be the same. But that doesn't mean it can't be amazing.

So many people allow themselves to be distracted along the way. They let their 'first world' problems get them down, losing perspective and getting sucked in by the everyday noise.

Useful belief is also a useful concept for teenagers to hold on to. Recently my son Jake had an opportunity to travel to Rwanda and Uganda as part of a school trip. It was an amazing experience for a 16-year-old boy. They were given the chance to visit schools, meet children at orphanages and visit museums to understand the horror of the civil war in Rwanda.

When Jake touched down in Uganda after the long trip from Australia, his bag arrived in baggage claim. Somehow it had been ripped open and his clothes were spilling out onto the conveyor belt. This would be stressful for a seasoned business traveller at Sydney airport, much less a teenager making his first overseas trip.

I got a text message from Jake that simply said:

> Dad I arrived safely in Uganda. A little hiccup as my bag was ripped open. No worries though. Was able to tape it up. No bags here at the airport. Will get a new bag when I can. #usefulbelief

Food for thought

1 Do you have a useful belief about the challenges in your life at the moment? If you were to change your belief to be more useful in those areas of your life, what would your new belief be?

2 What are the most useful actions for you to make a habit in order to get closer to being the person you want to be?

3 A useful belief is that everything that has happened to you happened for a reason. What are the things in your life that you need to move from being a source of pain to being a source of learning that has helped make you the person you are today? Bad things happen to good people. Think of useful ways to look at those bad things so they empower you instead of giving you pain.

Conclusion

Bringing it all together

This is an amazing time to be alive. It really is. Many of our elders remember life before television, while the younger generation has never known a world without instant connection through computer, tablet and phone. You can publish a version of yourself and put out your ideas on a live feed. This is exciting new territory!

At the same time, in our hyper-connected world there is so much to pay attention to. You can easily spend your entire day absorbed in videos on the internet or lost in social media. We are bombarded with every kind of information. Some of it is useful, well worth our paying attention to, while some of it is merely distracting and even a bit soul destroying if we let it be.

My goal in writing this book is to help readers work out what is important to them and to gain greater focus on how to spend their time in order to live more effectively. There is so much to look at and take in that it is vitally important to decide where to focus your attention!

One night recently I sat on a beach and marvelled at the force of the ocean as the waves crashed together. The thundering power of it always makes me reflect on how far that water has travelled before this wave reaches its destination. As I gazed up at a clear sky filled with shimmering starlight, I thought about how these natural forces are almost impossible to wrap your mind around.

It is so easy for us to miss the things in the world that are beautiful and important. It is a pretty cool thing that there are the right amounts of oxygen and gravity and all the other resources and forces that support our life on this planet. And what a planet! Think of the sunsets, sunrises, beaches, mountains, oceans, rivers, lakes, wildlife and forests, the turning of the seasons over thousands of years. It is truly awe-inspiring.

A sense of awe about the world is key to our humanity. The experience of being caught up in something bigger than ourselves gives a frame to our lives. It fills our lives with curiosity and joy. It is about the wonder of being human.

Our opportunities, and expectations, have never been greater. In this book I have introduced 10 steps that will help you to make the best of these opportunities.

My goal is to liberate you from the need to be perfect and from feelings of guilt when you fail to meet unreasonable expectations—and in this way to help you live a happier, healthier and more effective life. Here, in summary, are my

10 tools to 'cut the noise'. Think about these different tools and take away what resonates with you.

Perfection is not possible

We all strive to be perfect, and inevitably we fail to achieve that objective. In a hyper-connected world we broadcast the best version of ourselves for all to see. Be careful not to let that affect how you see yourself. The most important words you say are the words you say to yourself about yourself when you are by yourself. Most people are cruel in those moments.

This is about conscious awareness. The need for affirmation and the temptation to compare your life to others' is dangerous. Enjoy social media, but don't tie your sense of self-worth up in it. We are all out there doing the best we can. Trying to be perfect can consume us and get in the way of living an outstanding life.

10 seconds of guilt... move on!

You can't be all things to all people. Do the best you can and remember you are human. We all make mistakes. We all say stupid stuff. Be conscious of the feeling of guilt, but don't let it overwhelm you. Give it 10 seconds, then move on.

Recently I was presenting in Adelaide and had a conference call with a company in Sydney scheduled for 9:00 am.

At 8:15 I ducked down to the hotel restaurant for breakfast, leaving my phone on charge in my room. At 8:50 I walked back up to my room. Of course I had four missed calls, and only then remembered that 9:00 am in Adelaide is 9:30 in Sydney. I had missed the appointment. I called the client to apologise. She was great about my forgetting about the time change. I felt bad though, because there were four people on that call. It was an honest mistake and my intent was not bad. I hung up the phone, took a deep breath. There was nothing I could do about it—10 seconds of guilt... move on.

Circles of importance

Think about what activities and groups of people take up your time and identify your circles of importance. For most people there are six main areas in their lives that are really important. They will usually include family, work, friends, health, community and personal time. Put a circle around each of these groups. It is important to prioritise time for each circle, and also to determine which circle should have priority when the circles intersect, as they will.

Now think about the activities and people in your life that take up your time but don't fit in these circles. When faced with these time demands it is sometimes important to say no. We often get sucked into doing things that do not contribute to our circles of importance. Say no, and then, of course... 10 seconds of guilt!

Accelerated focus

Once you have identified a task that falls within your circles of importance, use accelerated focus to dial in and be fully present to work on that task. Studies show that people are more effective when they are focused on one thing than when they are trying to multi-task and achieve little focus.

The key to accelerated focus is being conscious of what the purpose of the task is. For a salesperson, for example, it may be prospecting. When you are attacking that prospect list, focus only on that and be consumed by it within the time frame you have decided on. If it is exercise, focus and be truly present throughout your workout to maximise your results. If it is spending time with your family, connect and be present with them without distraction.

Purpose

Knowing your purpose in everything you do will reduce or even eliminate the guilt. The story about my mom and her part in Operation Babylift in Vietnam illustrates this perfectly. Once she reconnected to her purpose, to why she was doing this in the first place, her guilt and fear evaporated.

Sometimes it is important to stop for a beat and think about why we are doing what we are doing. What drove us to do this to begin with? Is this activity serving our greater purpose? Sometimes, despite our accelerated focus on something within our circle of importance, we find we are actually focused on something that does not best serve that circle. We need to check back on our purpose every now and then.

Focus on the stumbling blocks

At my conferences people get excited by the new ideas I present to them. They write down all the goals and new behaviours they fully intend to put into action when they get back to the office. Often, though, they find that once in the flow of work again, they fall back into the same old routines, and those new goals and action lists are filed away in the saddest, loneliest place in the office—the repository of unactioned, unrealised conference notes, their yellowing pages ignored forever! It is one of the great frustrations of my work as a professional speaker.

To successfully create new habits or take effective action in goal setting, it is important first to focus on the stumbling blocks that may hold you back. It sounds counter-intuitive to focus on the negative, but studies show that people are more successful when they have a strategy for dealing with what might get in their way and block their progress.

It is easy to set a goal to go running on a beautiful sunny morning. It is the rainy day, when you are tempted to stay in bed, that you have to strategise for. Use a 'when, then' strategy: 'When it is likely to be raining in the morning, then I will put my alarm on the other side of the room and place my running shoes beneath it'. It is a simple preparation strategy to tackle the stumbling block so we do not fall back on our impulse to make a decision that does not support our goals. What are the stumbling blocks in your life? What holds you back at work? What are the distractions? Create a 'when, then' strategy to help you stay on target.

Frame it up—love, money and accomplishment

One of the downsides of living in a world that values instant gratification is that it becomes harder to do difficult tasks that aren't 'fun'. Recent studies indicate that many young people at work are convinced they can make a massive difference in the world within a short time frame. They have high expectations, believing they will progress quickly through the organisation and be rewarded handsomely for their efforts.

The problem, of course, is that when this doesn't happen they can become disillusioned. Menial tasks are not fun, and they believe they should be doing bigger and better things.

This is a tool to help with that. First, you need to recognise that not everything will be fun. This technique will help improve your accelerated focus on tasks that are not necessarily enjoyable. Most tasks can be classified into one of three frames: love, money and accomplishment. If the task is fun (family, friends, health, personal time), then it is about love. Enjoy it! If the task is about making money (work), it doesn't have to be fun. Ensure your accelerated focus is on the task at hand and why you are doing it (to earn money).

Sometimes a task is neither fun nor profitable, but it still needs to be done. Think of cleaning the refrigerator! Set your objective and roll up your sleeves. Not everything has to be enjoyable. We complain most when we think something should be fun but it's not. Set realistic expectations. There is a sense of accomplishment in finishing any task and doing it well.

Don't get too attached to the outcome

This does not mean we are not committed to the outcome. I will set myself targets and will do everything in my power to achieve them. In my experience, however, sometimes the best ideas, results and adaptations happen when I am not too attached to the outcome. Once I've completed the preparation and execution to the best of my ability, then, as my five-year-old son said, 'We'll see what we see'.

Not everything will go according to plan. Sometimes you meet someone who changes your view of what is important. Sometimes you become aware of better ideas that lead you down a different path. Sometimes it's just about enjoying yourself and realising that your original goal is no longer important. When you hold on too tight, you miss the enjoyment of what is actually happening. Just because it didn't finish the way you expected, it does not mean it's not better.

Which doesn't mean we don't set expectations. Executing a plan requires clear focus, vision and tenacity. It's like going for a hike. You head off down a track, and you are sure it is the route you intended to follow. But sometimes the track will fork, and some of the greatest adventures happen when you make an educated guess and turn off the beaten track.

Useful belief

It is important to make sure your belief systems support what you are trying to do. Ask yourself questions such as, 'What is the most useful thing to believe about this situation?' and 'What is the most useful thing I can do today to get me closer to where I want to be?'

Positive thinking doesn't work. The studies show that if you lie in bed in the morning and say to yourself, 'C'mon, just be positive today. You can do it!', when 10 o'clock rolls around and you can't sustain that positivity you actually feel worse about yourself than when you started.

Useful belief is pragmatic. It's practical. What are useful things to believe that support your goals? What useful actions can you take?

Core beliefs and identity

Think about the core beliefs that shape your life. What you truly believe in will drive your behaviour. Use your core beliefs to help you filter out all the external noise. It is so important to cut out the negative self-talk about your identity and get clear about what you want your identity to be. There are so many great words you can use to describe *you*: happy, joyful, friendly, enthusiastic, talented, attractive. There are also so many possible negative interpretations. It's easy to pick out the bad stuff if you want to.

What is useful for you to believe in? What is at the core of who you are as a human being? Clarity about who you are and what you represent will guide you through the tough decisions in your life. Remember, your identity will direct your behaviour. With an identity that serves you, the results can be amazing.

* * *

I hope you have enjoyed this book. I have deliberately presented these ideas in a simple, accessible form. I wanted to create a short book that could be picked up and read in one sitting—a quick experience, but one that leaves a lasting impression.

Finally, this book is about helping you to be kind to yourself on this journey called life. It is about being fully conscious and aware in your life, and working out how to make the most of the time you have. Communicate with yourself in a way that is kind. It is useful to be your own greatest friend. You will make mistakes—everyone does. That does not mean you have to beat yourself up about it for the rest of your life. That would not be useful.

Also available from Chris Helder...